All About Plants

All About

Seeds

Claire Throp

raintree

a Capstone company — publishers for children

Raintree is an imprint of Capstone Global Library Limited, a company incorporated in England and Wales having its registered office at 7 Pilgrim Street, London, EC4V 6LB – Registered company number: 6695582

www.raintreepublishers.co.uk
myorders@raintreepublishers.co.uk

Text © Capstone Global Library Limited 2015
First published in hardback in 2014
Paperback edition first published in 2015
The moral rights of the proprietor have been asserted.

Edited by Claire Throp and Brynn Baker
Designed by Peggie Carley
Picture research by Ruth Blair
Production by Victoria Fitzgerald
Originated by Capstone Global Library Ltd
Printed and bound in China by RR Donnelley Asia

ISBN 978 1 406 28440 9 (hardback)
18 17 16 15 14
10 9 8 7 6 5 4 3 2 1

ISBN 978 1 406 28446 1 (paperback)
19 18 17 16 15
10 9 8 7 6 5 4 3 2 1

British Library Cataloguing in Publication Data
A full catalogue record for this book is available from the British Library.

Acknowledgements
We would like to thank the following for permission to reproduce photographs: Alamy: Dirk v. Mallinckrodt, 18, 23 (middle); Getty Images: S.J. Krasemann, 19; Shutterstock: 2009fotofriends, 4, AlessandroZocc, back cover, 13, Charles Brutlag, 21, 23 (bottom), Daleen Loest, 16, Elenadesign, 10, Filipe B. Varela, 5, Jose Ignacio Soto, 22, Mazzzur, 8, 23 (top), Michal Zduniak, 15, Nikita Tiunov, 17, Photoexpert, 9, Pressmaster, 20, Rimantas Abromas, 7, Spiber, 6, sunsetman, 11, Thomas Klee, 12, Vitaly Ilyasov, 14; Superstock: Tips Images/Maurizio Polverelli, cover.

Every effort has been made to contact copyright holders of material reproduced in this book. Any omissions will be rectified in subsequent printings if notice is given to the publisher.

Contents

What are plants?

Plants are living things.

flower

stem

leaf

root

seed

Plants have
many parts.

What do plants need to grow?

Plants need sunlight and air to grow.

Plants need water to grow.

What are seeds?

seed

A seed is one part of a plant.
Flowers make seeds.

8

New plants grow from seeds.

Different seeds

seed

Some plants have lots
of small seeds.

seed

Some plants have big seeds.

Some seeds are round.

Some seeds have wings.

Spreading seeds

Some birds eat seeds.

These birds drop seeds
in new places.

The wind blows some seeds through the air.

The seeds land far away from
the old plant.

Some seeds burst out of **pods**.

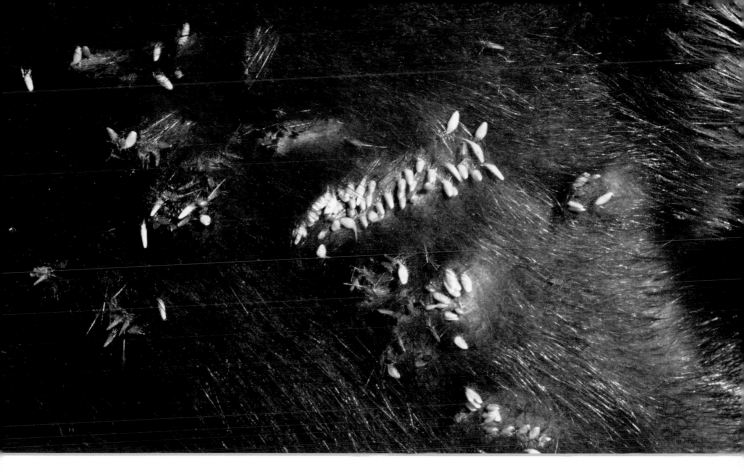

Some seeds hook onto animals' fur.
Animals carry seeds to new places.

How seeds grow

Seeds usually grow in the ground.

seed

root

They grow **roots**.

Plants need seeds

Seeds grow into new plants.

The new plants make new seeds.